Explore the Universe
OBSERVATORIES ON EARTH

WORLD
BOOK

a Scott Fetzer company

World Book, Inc.
233 N. Michigan Avenue
Chicago, IL 60601
U.S.A.

For information about other World Book publications, visit our
Web site at **http://www.worldbookonline.com** or call
1-800-WORLDBK (967-5325).

For information about sales to schools and
libraries, call **1-800-975-3250 (United States)**,
or **1-800-837-5365 (Canada)**.

Library of Congress Cataloging-in-Publication data
Observatories on Earth.
    p. cm. -- (Explore the universe)
    Summary: "An introduction to observatories on Earth with
information about their history and use. Includes diagrams,
fun facts, glossary, resource list, and index"--Provided by
publisher.
    Includes index.
    ISBN 978-0-7166-9553-0
    1. Astronomical observatories--Juvenile literature.
    2. Telescopes--Juvenile literature. I. World Book, Inc.
    QB81.O2665 2010
    522'.1--dc22

                        2009042608

ISBN 978-0-7166-9544-8 (set)
Printed in China at Leo Paper Products, LTD.,
    Heshan, Guangdong
1st printing February 2010

STAFF

Executive Committee:
President: Paul A. Gazzolo
Vice President and Chief Marketing Officer:
    Patricia Ginnis
Vice President and Chief Financial Officer:
    Donald D. Keller
Vice President and Editor in Chief: Paul A. Kobasa
Vice President, Licensing & Business Development:
    Richard Flower
Managing Director, International: Benjamin Hinton
Director, Human Resources: Bev Ecker
Chief Technology Officer: Tim Hardy

Editorial:
Associate Director, Supplementary Publications:
    Scott Thomas
Managing Editor, Supplementary Publications:
    Barbara A. Mayes
Senior Editor, Supplementary Publications:
    Kristina A. Vaicikonis
Manager, Research, Supplementary Publications:
    Cheryl Graham
Manager, Contracts & Compliance
    (Rights & Permissions): Loranne K. Shields
Editors: Michael DuRoss, Brian Johnson
Writer: Darlene Stille
Indexer: David Pofelski

Graphics and Design:
Manager: Tom Evans
Coordinator, Design Development
    and Production: Brenda B. Tropinski
Senior Designer: Isaiah Sheppard
Photographs Editor: Kathy Creech

Pre-Press and Manufacturing:
Director: Carma Fazio
Manufacturing Manager: Steven K. Hueppchen
Production/Technology Manager: Anne Fritzinger
Proofreader: Emilie Schrage

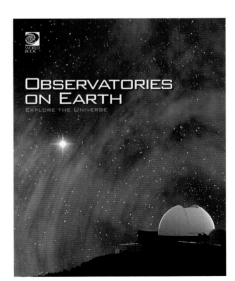

Cover image:
A star-filled sky dominated
by Venus, the brighest object
in the night sky, frames one
of the observatories at the
Haleakala High Altitude
Observatory Site on the
island of Maui in Hawaii
in a combined photograph
and artist's illustration.
The summit of Mount
Haleakala, which is about
10,000 feet (3,000 meters)
above sea level, sits above
about one-third of Earth's
atmosphere.

© Bill Brooks, Masterfile

CONTENTS

If a word is printed in **bold letters that look like this,** that word's
meaning is given in the glossary on pages 60-61.

INTRODUCTION

People have always studied the heavens. They have watched the sun appear in the east, rise through the sky, and set in the west. They have watched the moon wax and wane each month, and they have seen the stars drift slowly across the night sky. For thousands of years, people have grappled with the mysteries of the sky.

Modern observatories have come a long way from the towers used by ancient people to study the sky. Modern observatories enable astronomers to study the universe. Astronomers have discovered that the sun is only one of trillions of stars. They have learned that the universe is about 13.7 billion years old. They have even discovered distant worlds in orbit around other stars. They have discovered that the universe is more magnificent than ancient astronomers ever dreamed possible.

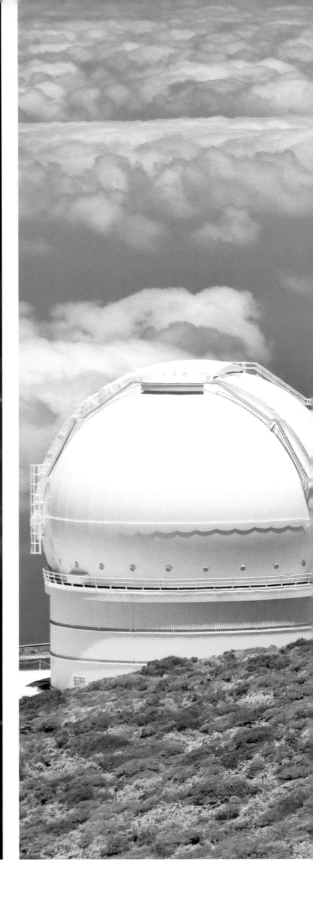

The Gran Telescopio Canarias has one of the largest mirrors of any visible and infrared light telescope. Its *primary* (main) mirror measures 34 feet (10.4 meters) in diameter. The telescope is on the island of La Palma in Spain's Canary Islands.

From the ancient Babylonians to the Egyptians, Chinese, and Maya, civilization and astronomy have developed hand in hand.

ADVANCED ANCIENTS

The ancient Babylonians, who lived in what is now southern Iraq from about 2000 to 200 B.C., founded the science of astronomy. Astronomy is the systematic study of objects in the sky. The Babylonians also built the first **observatories,** buildings for observing the heavens. They created the first **star** catalogs, which described stars and **constellations.** They used mathematics to predict eclipses of the moon, the movement of **planets** across the sky, and the length of days and nights.

MARKING THE SOLSTICE

Many ancient people believed that the stars were actually gods, ruling over Earth from the heavens. But ancient astronomy had its practical side, too.

Some of the earliest structures helped people mark the summer **solstice.** The summer solstice is the longest day of the year and marks the beginning of summer. Such observatories helped ancient people know when to plant their crops.

Stonehenge in southern England lines up with sunrise on the summer solstice and sunset on the winter solstice. A temple

On the summer solstice, the stones of Stonehenge align with the rising sun.

at Machu Picchu in Peru features a special opening that allows sunlight to shine through only on the day of the summer solstice.

COSMIC CALENDARS

Many ancient people, including the Egyptians, Babylonians, and Maya, used astronomy to create calendars. We take calendars for granted today, but tracking the days of the year was a major achievement for ancient people. They used the movements of the moon, the planets, and the sun to create their calendars. They used the calendars to plan religious ceremonies and to keep track of planting and harvest times.

Stonehenge, built beginning in about 3100 B.C., still stands in England.

Ancient observatories are among the oldest surviving structures built by human beings. Many ancient people studied the heavens for religious reasons, but these observatories had a practical side, too. Ancient people used their observations to create the first calendars. Such calendars told farmers when to plant their crops, increasing the chances for a good harvest. Astronomy became the earliest systematic investigation of the natural world—the first science.

The Great Hypostyle Hall of Karnak near Luxor, Egypt, may have been used by the ancient Egyptians for 2,000 years to track the motion of the stars. ▶

◀ **The Chinese used a brass "celestial globe," made in A.D. 1439, to track the movements of the stars.**

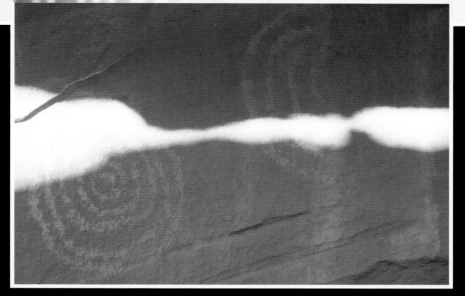

◄ At sunrise on the summer solstice, sunlight illuminates markings called petroglyphs on a rock ledge at Hovenweep National Monument in Arizona.

A ruined tower at Hovenweep National Monument may have been an ancient observatory used by the ancestral Puebloans, a Native American group that flourished from about A.D. 500 to 1300.

▼

CHICHÉN ITZÁ— ARCHITECTURE AND THE GODS

The Maya observatory at Chichén Itzá on the Yucatán Peninsula of Mexico shows the great achievements ancient people made in studying the heavens. Chichén Itzá was an important regional capital that reached the height of its power from about A.D. 900 to 1200. The city was also an important center of Maya astronomy.

THE CASTLE

The tallest building in Chichén Itzá is a large pyramid dedicated to a feathered snake god called Kukulkan. The pyramid is nicknamed "the castle." On the spring and fall equinoxes—when day and night are both 12 hours long—shadows from the pyramid's stepped terraces combine to create the image of a shadowy snake. As the sun sets, the snake seems to wiggle down the stairway (below).

The shadow of a snake representing the god Kukulkan (above) appears to slither down the steps of the pyramid at Chichén Itzá (right).

◀ The castle also has four sets of stairs representing the four seasons. Each has 91 steps. Together, they total 364 steps, the approximate number of days it takes Earth to orbit the sun.

▲

From El Caracol, priests, who also served as astronomers, observed the sky.

El Caracol is aligned with the movements of the planet Venus, which was associated with the feathered snake god Kukulkan.

▼

THE OBSERVATORY

Scientists believe that a tower in Chichén Itzá called El Caracol served as the city's astronomical observatory. The tower is aligned with the motions of the planet Venus, with narrow windows that mark the northern and southern points of Venus's yearly path across the evening sky. Venus was very important to the Maya. The planet was associated with the snake god Kukulkan, who was worshiped at Chichén Itzá.

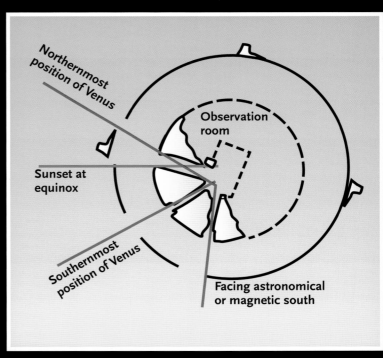

Northernmost position of Venus

Observation room

Sunset at equinox

Southernmost position of Venus

Facing astronomical or magnetic south

HOW DO MODERN OBSERVATORIES DIFFER FROM ANCIENT OBSERVATORIES?

The accomplishments of ancient astronomers are impressive, especially considering that they relied only on the unaided human eye to gather light from the **stars.** When astronomers added telescopes to **observatories,** they opened a new realm of science. Today, telescopes, computers, and other advanced technology have enabled astronomers to probe the depths of space and time.

TELESCOPES

The telescope is the heart of a modern observatory. A telescope is an instrument that **magnifies** distant objects. The invention of telescopes in the 1600's brought great advances in our understanding of the universe. Today, the most powerful telescopes can detect images about 1 million times fainter than those visible to the unaided eye.

RECORDING IMAGES

The ability to record images is another advantage of modern observatories. Taking pictures allows many scientists to study the same image, even years after it was recorded. Also, if film is exposed to a dim object for a long time, a bright picture results. In this way, a photograph may reveal many details that cannot be seen by a person using the telescope directly.

The Danish astronomer Tycho Brahe (1546-1601) was among the last astronomers who made observations using the unaided eye rather than a telescope. His observations were far more precise than those of earlier astronomers.

COMPUTERS

Computers are another important tool used by astronomers. Computers help astronomers record and analyze the flood of data produced by modern observatories. They are able to analyze **electromagnetic radiation** that is invisible to human beings. Computers allow observatories to record and analyze millions of images, and they help telescopes to track the movement of stars.

TASTE THE STARS

Some instruments in modern observatories would baffle ancient people. For example, a spectrometer, breaks light down into all the colors of the rainbow, which is called the **spectrum.** The spectrum given off by a heavenly object reveals the different **chemical elements** of which it is made. It is almost as if astronomers can reach out and sample the chemistry of stars in deep space.

A scientist records light from a heavenly object using a sophisticated camera, one of many technologically advanced devices used in modern observatories.

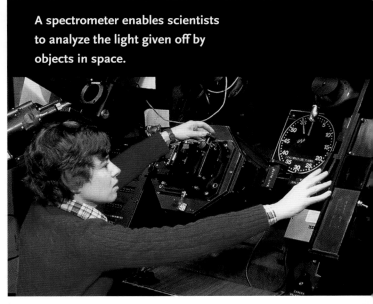

A spectrometer enables scientists to analyze the light given off by objects in space.

DID YOU KNOW?

Binoculars are two small telescopes joined together in a way that produces a three-dimensional image.

The telescopes and other instruments in modern **observatories** are delicate technology that must be protected from harsh weather. By enclosing a telescope in a dome, astronomers can protect the telescope from the elements. Yet a telescope that could examine only one spot in the sky would be of little use. Today's telescopes can be turned so that astronomers can observe the entire sky.

THE DOME

The dome of an astronomical observatory is usually made of metal. It fits on the base of an observatory like a lid fits on a jar. The dome sits on rollers or wheels that move it around a track on the base. Small domes can be turned by hand. Machinery turns large domes.

The dome features a narrow slit covered by metal doors. To use the telescope, astronomers open the metal doors covering the slit. By tilting the telescope and rotating the dome, astronomers can point the telescope wherever they wish.

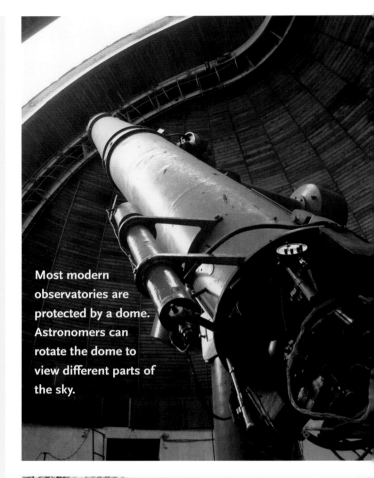

Most modern observatories are protected by a dome. Astronomers can rotate the dome to view different parts of the sky.

Founded in 1675, the Royal Observatory at Greenwich, United Kingdom, was among the earliest modern observatories. It was established to locate the positions of the stars, moon, and sun more accurately and so improve navigation by the British Royal Navy.

THE MOUNTING

The first telescopes fit easily in a person's hand, but the largest telescopes today weigh many thousands of tons. A modern telescope rests on complex machinery called the **mounting.** The mounting turns the telescope and controls its tilt. The mounting also allows the telescope to turn with the Earth's rotation. This ability to turn allows the telescope to stay focused on one spot in the sky all night long.

The Sphinx Observatory (below) in the Alps in Switzerland is the highest sky observatory on Earth. A dome protects the delicate machinery inside.

TWINKLE LESS, LITTLE STAR

On a starlit night, we might gaze up at the **stars** and admire how they twinkle. For astronomers, the twinkling of stars is a serious problem.

Stars twinkle because of **atmospheric distortion.** In fact, stars don't really twinkle at all. Instead, pockets of moving air and water vapor in Earth's atmosphere act like **lenses,** bending starlight as it travels to the ground. This atmospheric distortion can make objects viewed through a telescope appear blurry.

INTO THIN AIR

One way to reduce distortion is to climb a mountain. The higher you go, the thinner the air gets. The thickest part of the atmosphere is concentrated at the lowest altitudes. By building observatories on top of mountains, astronomers can escape the worst of atmospheric distortion. The only way to eliminate distortion completely is to put telescopes into space.

IRONING OUT THE TWINKLES

Scientists have also developed technology that can correct atmospheric distortion. This technology is called **adaptive optics.** It works by measuring the air's distortion. This information is processed by computers to determine how a telescope's mirror must be adjusted to compensate for the distortion. Tiny mechanical parts can then bend the mirror to correct the atmospheric distortion to some degree.

A laser beam aimed into the sky helps astronomers map the distortion of light caused by the atmosphere. Astronomers use this information as part of a system called adaptive optics to help focus the telescope in a way that eliminates the distortion.

Earth's atmosphere distorts the light from heavenly objects. Placing observatories on mountains lifts them above the thickest part of the atmosphere, allowing for clearer images.

The effects of atmospheric distortion are clear in photographs of moonset taken from Earth's orbit. As the moon sinks below the horizon, its image becomes increasingly distorted as the atmosphere grows thicker.

Jupiter's moon Io appears in ▶ much greater detail in images taken by the Keck Telescope using adaptive optics (right, top and bottom) than in an image made without the technology (far right, bottom). The images made using adaptive optics almost rival an image of Io taken by the Jupiter probe Galileo from a much closer distance (far right, top).

The first telescopes were somewhat like enormous magnifying glasses pointed up at the sky. Most telescopes are still **optical,** which means that they observe **visible light.** However, other telescopes measure invisible light, such as **infrared rays** or **radio waves.**

THE GREATER RAINBOW

The first astronomers did not know that human beings see only a narrow range of light. Visible light is a kind of **electromagnetic radiation** given off by the sun and other **stars.** However, visible light makes up only a small part of light's total **spectrum.**

Light travels through space as long or short waves. The **wavelength** of light is the distance from the *crest* (top) of one wave to the next. Radio waves, **microwaves,** and infrared rays are light with wavelengths longer than those of visible light. **Ultraviolet, X rays,** and **gamma rays** are light with wavelengths shorter than visible light.

A composite image of the Pinwheel Galaxy combines different parts of the spectrum, including X rays, visible light, and infrared, shown individually below.

X rays reveal exploded stars and energy near black holes.

Visible light reveals stars and clouds of dust and gas.

Infrared light reveals heat from areas where stars are forming.

Observatories house different kinds of telescopes. Some telescopes observe visible light. Others gather forms of electromagnetic radiation that are invisible to people.

THE INVISIBLE UNIVERSE

Scientists have built telescopes that observe different forms of light. On the ground, radio telescopes and infrared telescopes have provided powerful new tools to astronomers. Infrared telescopes may look much like optical telescopes. Radio telescopes look like giant satellite dishes. Infrared and radio telescopes are especially useful because such light passes through dust and gas, which block visible light.

Earth's atmosphere blocks ultraviolet light, X rays, and gamma rays. As a result, telescopes that measure this part of the spectrum must be lifted higher into the atmosphere in airplanes or launched into space.

WHAT RADIATION REVEALS

Name	Sources
X rays	The sun's corona; disks of material around black holes; quasars
Visible light	Planets; stars; galaxies; asteroids; comets
Infrared waves	Stars in the process of forming; relatively cool stars; planets

A VERY LONG FLIGHT

The New Horizons space probe is traveling to Pluto at about 12 miles (20 kilometers) per second, or about 45,000 miles (72,000 kilometers) per hour. The figures below* describe how long it would take this probe to reach different parts of the universe.

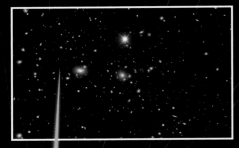

The Andromeda Galaxy is only 2.3 million light-years away, but the probe would need 34 billion years to reach it.

The Coma Supercluster is a group of galaxies 300 million light-years away. The probe would need 4.5 trillion years to reach these galaxies. By then, all the stars would have burned out.

* These figures are based on the distance to these objects today. They do not account for the expansion of the universe.

The distance between Earth and Jupiter varies as these planets orbit the sun, but at their closest, the probe would need about a year to reach Jupiter.

Astronomers have observed light that traveled more than 13 billion years from galaxies that existed early in the history of the universe. This light began its journey when the universe was young.

Space is vast. The nearest **star** to the sun is called Proxima Centauri. It is about 24.7 trillion miles (39.7 trillion kilometers) away. If you could somehow take an airliner to Proxima Centauri, the flight would last more than 4 million years.

THE SPEED OF LIGHT

Because space is vast, astronomers measure distance in special units called **light-years.** A light-year is the distance that light travels in one year. Nothing in the universe is faster than light, which travels at the speed of 186,282 miles (299,792 kilometers) per second. Light is fast enough to circle the Earth more than seven times in one second. At this speed, light can travel about 5.88 trillion miles (9.46 trillion kilometers) in one year. Thus, astronomers say that Proxima Centauri is 4.2 light-years away.

BACK IN TIME

Stars more distant than our nearest neighbors may be thousands, millions, or even billions of light-years away. When we observe a star that is 1,000 light-years away, we are observing the star as it was when light left it 1,000 years ago. The star could explode tomorrow, and we would not know for 1,000 years. Thus, when we observe objects in deep space, we look back in time.

THE OUTER LIMITS

Light from the most distant **galaxies** we have observed traveled more than 13.5 billion light-years. When the light left those galaxies, the universe was less than a billion years old. With more powerful telescopes, astronomers will be able to observe more distant galaxies, from even further back in time. They may someday peer back to the first stars.

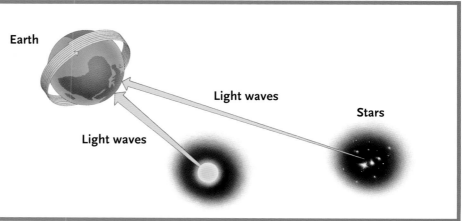

Light travels so fast that a wave can circle the Earth about seven times per second. Even at that speed, light needs 8 minutes to travel from the sun to the Earth and 4.2 years to reach us from the nearest star other than the sun.

Earth

Light waves

Light waves

Stars

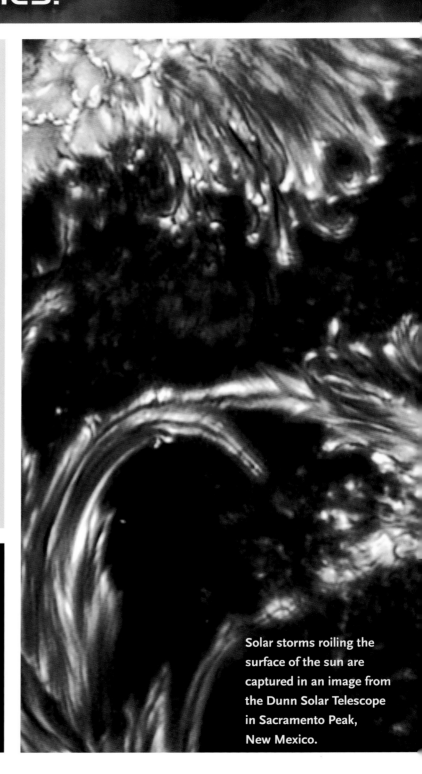

THE LOCAL NEIGHBORHOOD

Astronomers use ground-based **observatories** to study the sun and the **planets** of the **solar system.** By studying the sun, astronomers hope to learn about **stars** in general. They also study solar storms that can affect electronic devices and systems in orbit and on Earth. A program called Spaceguard uses telescopes to search for objects that might strike Earth.

OTHER WORLDS

Astronomers also use ground-based observatories to search for planets around other stars. They have already found more than 400 of these exoplanets. The next generation of telescopes will help in this search. The mirrors of the largest ground-based **optical** telescopes today are about 33 feet (10 meters) across.

DID YOU KNOW?

Parts for the Snow Solar Telescope, the first telescope built at the Mount Wilson Observatory in California, had to be carried up the steep mountainside by pack mules in 1904 and 1905.

Solar storms roiling the surface of the sun are captured in an image from the Dunn Solar Telescope in Sacramento Peak, New Mexico.

Astronomers use ground-based observatories to study the Sun, planets, and other objects in the solar system. They also study stars, galaxies, and other objects in deep space.

Ground-based telescopes under construction will feature mirrors three times as large.

THE GREAT BEYOND
Astronomers use telescopes on the ground to study distant stars and clouds of gas. They have peered into the center of our **galaxy** and studied the life cycle of stars. Astronomers have studied our local group of galaxies and surveyed the structure of the universe. As telescopes become more powerful, scientists can observe more of the universe.

A comet-like cloud of dust and gas with a tail about 8 light-years long crosses the Milky Way in an image taken by the Victor M. Blanco Telescope in Chile. The cloud contains enough material to make several stars the size of the sun.

THE MECHANICAL EYE

Astronomers have developed many kinds of telescopes, but **optical** telescopes remain the most common. These telescopes, which collect **visible light,** are also the oldest kind of telescope.

In many ways, an optical telescope resembles the human eye. Both detect the same part of the electromagnetic **spectrum**—visible light. When light enters the human eye, a **lens** focuses the image onto the back of the eye, where nerves send signals to the brain. In the most basic kind of optical telescope, a series of lenses focuses the image. The image can be directed at an **eyepiece.** This is an opening on the telescope that allows a person to view the image directly. In other cases, the telescope focuses the light on electronics that record the image.

ANATOMY OF A TELESCOPE

Optical telescopes include several basic parts. One part is the tube that forms the body of the telescope. The main light-gathering part of an optical telescope is called the **objective.**

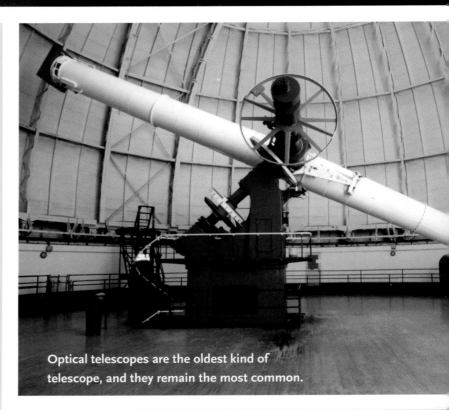

Optical telescopes are the oldest kind of telescope, and they remain the most common.

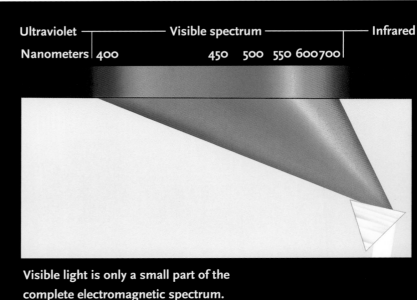

Ultraviolet — Visible spectrum — Infrared

Nanometers | 400   450   500   550 600 700

Visible light is only a small part of the complete electromagnetic spectrum.

An optical telescope is a tube-shaped instrument that uses visible light to magnify objects in the heavens.

In one type of optical telescope, the objective is a lens. These telescopes use **refraction** to focus the image. Refraction is the process of bending or changing the direction of a light ray. In other types, the objective is a mirror. These telescopes use **reflection** to focus the image. Reflection is the process of causing a light ray to bounce off a surface. Still other telescopes use a combination of reflection and refraction.

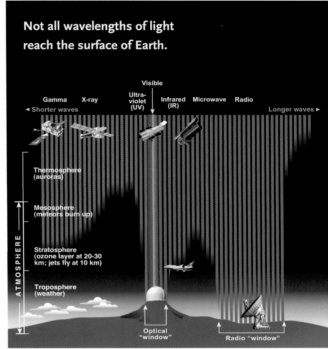

Not all wavelengths of light reach the surface of Earth.

Gamma   X-ray   Ultra-violet (UV)   Visible   Infrared (IR)   Microwave   Radio

◄ Shorter waves   Longer waves ►

ATMOSPHERE

Thermosphere (auroras)

Mesosphere (meteors burn up)

Stratosphere (ozone layer at 20-30 km; jets fly at 10 km)

Troposphere (weather)

Optical "window"

Radio "window"

The Yerkes Observatory in Wisconsin houses the largest refracting telescope in the world.

KECK OBSERVATORY— AT THE EDGE OF THE HEAVENS

The two telescopes at the Keck Observatory, established in the mid-1990's, sit high atop Mauna Kea, an inactive volcano in Hawaii. The huge segmented-mirror telescopes each weigh 300 tons (272 metric tons). They are the second most powerful optical telescopes in the world, slightly behind the Gran Telescopio Canarias on the Canary Islands. The Keck telescopes can gather *infrared* (heat) as well as visible light. Astronomers using the Keck telescopes have studied the solar system and analyzed radiation from the most distant galaxies. Keck astronomers have also discovered planets around other stars.

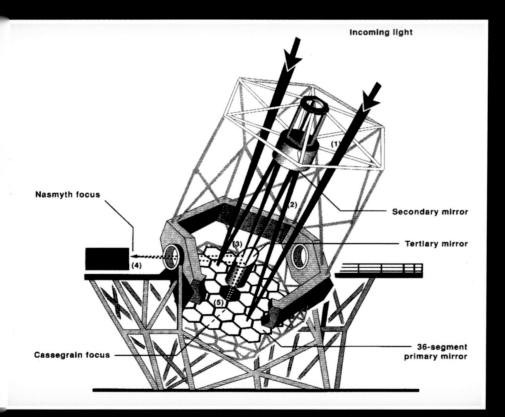

Incoming light

Nasmyth focus

Secondary mirror

Tertiary mirror

(1)
(2)
(3)
(4)
(5)

Cassegrain focus

36-segment
primary mirror

Each dome of the Keck Observatory houses a telescope that is eight stories tall. The telecopes gather light using primary mirrors made up of 36 segments. Combined, the segments act as a single mirror 33 feet (10 meters) across. If the telescopes housed a single mirror rather than segments, their tremendous weight would have caused the mirrors to sag, distorting images.

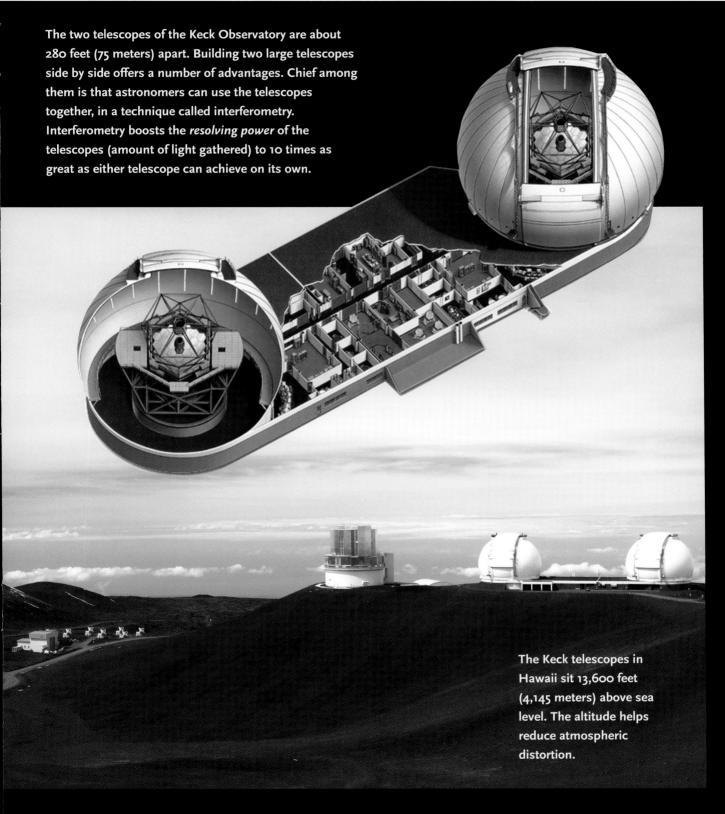

The two telescopes of the Keck Observatory are about 280 feet (75 meters) apart. Building two large telescopes side by side offers a number of advantages. Chief among them is that astronomers can use the telescopes together, in a technique called interferometry. Interferometry boosts the *resolving power* of the telescopes (amount of light gathered) to 10 times as great as either telescope can achieve on its own.

The Keck telescopes in Hawaii sit 13,600 feet (4,145 meters) above sea level. The altitude helps reduce atmospheric distortion.

WHAT ARE MAGNIFICATION AND RESOLVING POWER?

ZOOMING IN

The most important measures of a telescope's power are its **magnification** and its **resolving power.**

Magnification makes small objects appear larger. A telescope's magnification is expressed as a number followed by an X. For example, 7X magnification means the image will be seven times as large as the unaided eye can see. At higher magnification, a telescope must be held very steady, so the enlarged images do not jump or vibrate.

The magnification of a telescope is based on its **focal length,** or the distance from the **objective** to the **focal plane.** The objective is the **lens** or mirror used to gather light. The focal plane is the area where the image forms.

RESOLUTION IS KING

Resolving power, also called resolution, is the amount of light a telescope gathers. It determines how clear an image will be.

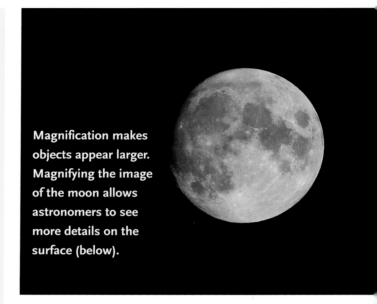

Magnification makes objects appear larger. Magnifying the image of the moon allows astronomers to see more details on the surface (below).

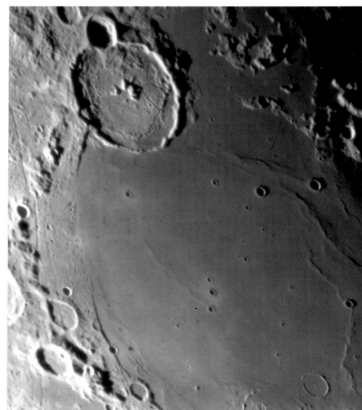

Magnification makes small objects appear larger. Resolving power is the amount of light a telescope can gather.

Resolution is ultimately more important than magnification. A telescope with high magnification and low resolution might produce an image of a **star** as a blob of light. A telescope with high resolution might show that the blob is actually two stars. Higher resolution first revealed that distant **galaxies** are made up of individual stars, and it enables telescopes to detect dim objects.

MONSTER OBJECTIVES

A telescope's resolving power depends upon the amount of light its objective **lens** or mirror is able to gather. A larger objective will gather more light. The size of the objective is called its **aperture.** Improvements to telescopes have largely depended upon increased aperture.

Today, amateur **optical** telescopes can gather about 100 times as much light as the unaided eye. In contrast, Galileo's telescopes could gather about 30 times as much light. Large modern telescopes can gather about 1 million times as much light as the unaided eye.

The Horsehead Nebula appears in far greater detail in an image made by an optical telescope in 2008 (above) than it does in the first photograph of this massive cloud of dust and gas (below), taken in 1888.

In 1608, Hans Lippershey of the Netherlands used his skill in making **lenses** for eyeglasses to invent the first telescope. The telescope was an instant success, especially among military leaders who were eager to use it to observe distant enemies. In 1609, the Italian mathematician and astronomer Galileo Galilei read descriptions of the telescope. He decided to build his own.

NEW AND IMPROVED

The telescope invented by Lippershey could **magnify** objects only about three times as much as the unaided eye, or 3X. Galileo soon improved the design. Eventually, Galileo's telescopes achieved magnification near 30X. All of the first telescopes were **refraction** telescopes that used lenses to focus the image.

DID YOU KNOW?

Caroline Lucretia Herschel, the first famous woman astronomer, used telescopes that she and her brother William built to discover many comets and objects that later astronomers learned were galaxies.

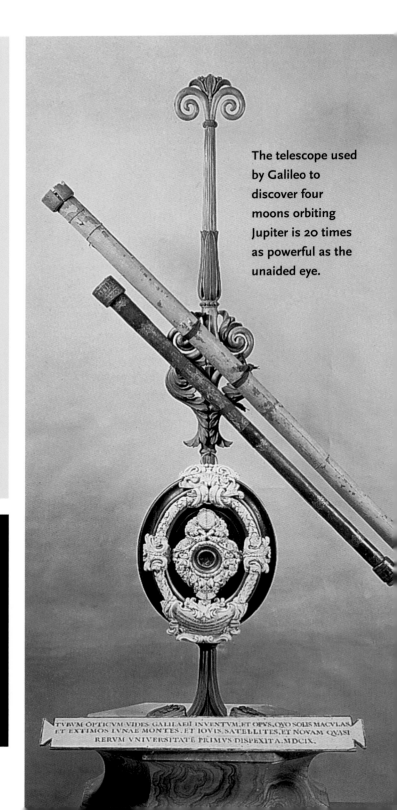

The telescope used by Galileo to discover four moons orbiting Jupiter is 20 times as powerful as the unaided eye.

TVBVM OPTICVM VIDES GALILAEI INVENTVM, ET OPVS, QVO SOLIS MACVLAS ET EXTIMOS LVNAE MONTES, ET IOVIS SATELLITES, ET NOVAM QVASI RERVM VNIVERSITATÉ PRIMVS DISPEXIT A. MDCIX.

GALILEAN MOONS

When Galileo pointed his telescope at the heavens, he began a new age of astronomy and science. He discovered that far from being smooth, the moon is covered by mountains and craters.

In 1610, he discovered four moons orbiting Jupiter. These were the first moons to be discovered around other **planets**. These four moons are still called Galilean moons in his honor. He also found that the white band across the middle of the night sky that we know as the Milky Way is made up of individual **stars.**

Galileo demonstrates his telescope, which he called an "optick tube," to officials in the Italian city of Venice on Aug. 25, 1609, as shown in an engraving from the 1600's. At the presentation, Galileo stressed the military benefits of the instrument.

NEW MOONS, NEW WONDERS

Galileo Galilei, who turned his telescope on the heavens for the first time in 1609, has been called the founder of modern experimental science. Among other discoveries, Galileo found the four largest moons of Jupiter, now named Io, Europa, Ganymede, and Callisto. These moons are sometimes called "Galilean moons" in his honor. Galileo was also the first person to view the rings of Saturn, though his telescope was not powerful enough for him to make out the shape of the rings. These and other observations deepened Galileo's conviction that Polish astronomer Nicolaus Copernicus was correct in claiming that all planets, including Earth, orbit the sun. For thousands of years, Europeans had believed Earth was the center of the universe. Today, we know that all planets orbit the sun, which itself orbits the center of our galaxy.

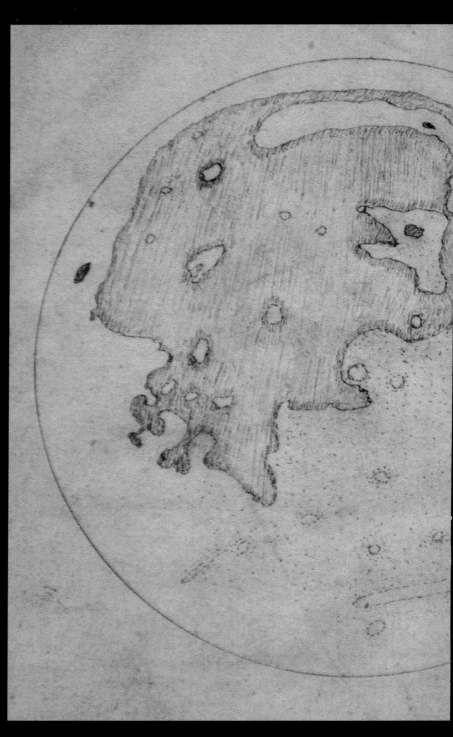

A map of the moon drawn by amateur ▶ English astronomer Thomas Harriot on July 26, 1609, suggests that he was the first to view the moon through a telescope, rather than Galileo. Harriot did not publish his map until several years after Galileo published his drawings of the lunar surface.

◀ Galileo's sketch of the moon, which was published in December 1609, has long been considered historical proof that he was the first to view the moon through a telescope. But Harriot's map apparently predated Galileo's.

Galileo was the first astronomer ▶ to see the rings of Saturn. At his first viewing in 1610, he thought the rings were large moons on either side of the planet (right, top). When Galileo observed the rings again in 1616 (right, bottom), Saturn had changed position relative to the Earth, allowing him to make out what he described as "arms." It was not until nearly 50 years later that more powerful telescopes enabled the Dutch astronomer Christiaan Huygens to correctly describe the rings.

HOW DOES A REFRACTING TELESCOPE WORK?

The first telescopes were all **refracting** telescopes. These telescopes revolutionized the study of the heavens.

BENDING LIGHT

The tube of a refracting telescope has a large **lens** at one end. This lens is the **objective** that gathers light. The lens objective is a **convex** lens, which means that the center of the objective lens is thicker than its edges. As light passes through the objective, the glass slows down the light. The light slows the most in the thick, central part of the objective lens. It slows the least in the thin glass at the edges. In this way, the lens bends the light so that it forms an image—a picture of the object—inside the telescope on the **focus.** The light from this image then goes through another lens, called the **eyepiece,** at the small end of the telescope. The eyepiece bends the light again and makes the object look big.

Refracting telescopes are the oldest kind of telescope, and many people continue to use them today.

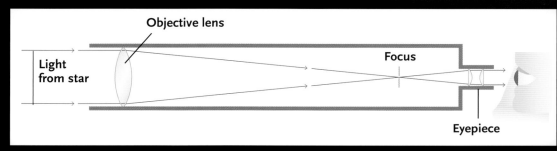

Light from star · Objective lens · Focus · Eyepiece

Refracting telescopes use convex lenses that gather and focus light.

RENEGADE RAINBOWS

Unfortunately, the first refracting telescopes had a serious flaw. As light passes through the lens, the glass slows different parts of the **spectrum** at different rates. For example, it slows violet light much more than it slows red light. This effect caused the first telescopes to produce images with rainbow coloring around the edges. This rainbow edging is called **chromatic aberration.**

THE CURE IS WORSE

Astronomers tried to solve the problem by using convex lenses with less curvature. These lenses reduce chromatic aberration. But the length of the tube from the lens to the focus had to be much longer. To achieve this longer **focal length**, astronomers began to build refracting telescopes that were as long as 200 feet (60 meters). That's equal to the length of five school buses.

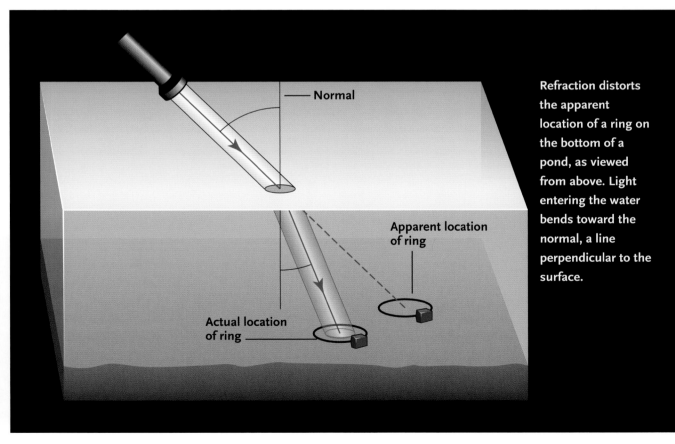

Normal

Apparent location of ring

Actual location of ring

Refraction distorts the apparent location of a ring on the bottom of a pond, as viewed from above. Light entering the water bends toward the normal, a line perpendicular to the surface.

Beginning with the invention of the first telescope, astronomers have pursued more powerful instruments. There have been many challenges along the way, including the sheer mechanical effort of turning large, heavy telescopes to observe different parts of the sky. Perhaps the most daunting challenge was building and polishing ever-larger mirrors that could gather more light. Even today, scientists are hard at work building larger telescopes.

The astronomer William Herschel ▶ built a 48-inch (120-centimeter) reflecting telescope in the United Kingdom between 1785 and 1789. The telescope was 40 feet (12 meters) long.

◀ The Leviathan of Parsontown, built in 1845 in Ireland by the Earl of Rosse (William Parsons), an Irish astronomer, remained the largest telescope in the world for several decades. The Leviathan had a 72-inch (1.8-meter) mirror. Parsons is credited with many discoveries, including describing the Crab Nebula and being the first to identify the spiral shape of "nebulae" that we now know are spiral galaxes.

American astronomer Edwin Hubble poses in the 200-inch (5-meter) Hale Telescope at the Mount Palomar Observatory in California, shortly before his death in 1953. The Hale was the most powerful telescope from 1948 to 1993. Using the smaller 100-inch (2.5-meter) Hooker Telescope at Mt. Wilson Observatory, also in California, Hubble revolutionized astronomy in the 1920's. He proved that the Andromeda Nebula was actually a separate galaxy far beyond the Milky Way. He also discovered that the farther apart galaxies are from each other, the faster they move away from each other. This movement is caused by the expansion of the universe.

WHO INVENTED THE FIRST REFLECTING TELESCOPE?

Refracting telescopes changed astronomy forever, but their **convex lenses** caused problems. **Reflecting** telescopes do not have these problems because they use mirrors instead of lenses.

THE RACE TO REFLECT

The first reflecting telescope was built by Italian astronomer Niccolo Zucchi in 1616, but this telescope did not work well. Scottish mathematician and astronomer James Gregory published a design for a reflector in 1663, but he could not find a craftsman who could build it. It was not until the English astronomer and mathematician Sir Isaac Newton built a reflector in 1668 that the potential of these telescopes was realized.

FROM COLOR TO COSMOS

Newton conducted research into the colors that make up **visible light.** He used a **prism,** a piece of glass cut to have several flat sides. Light passing through a prism breaks into the colors of the rainbow, because the glass

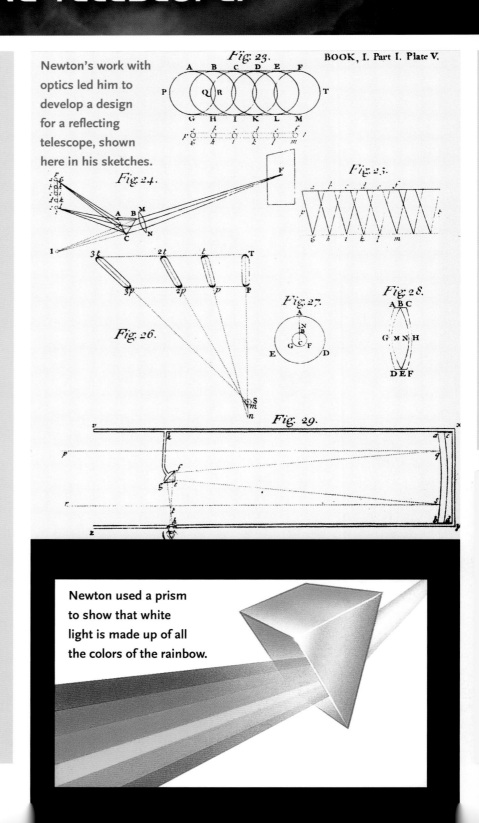

Newton's work with optics led him to develop a design for a reflecting telescope, shown here in his sketches.

Newton used a prism to show that white light is made up of all the colors of the rainbow.

bends the light according to its **wavelength.** The same effect causes a rainbow effect called **chromatic aberration** around images taken by refractor telescopes.

Unlike lenses, mirrors do not bend light but bounce light off the surface. Newton realized that a telescope built with mirrors would not produce chromatic aberration. Newton's reflecting telescope became the instrument of choice for astronomers.

SAGGING OBJECTIVES

Mirrors offer other advantages as well. More powerful telescopes require larger **objectives** to gather light. However, larger lenses are thick and heavy. Eventually, a large lens becomes so heavy that it bends and warps under its own weight, distorting the image. By contrast, mirrors are flat. They can be made larger without greatly increasing their weight. Reflecting telescopes allowed for enormous improvements in **resolving power,** as their mirrors grew larger.

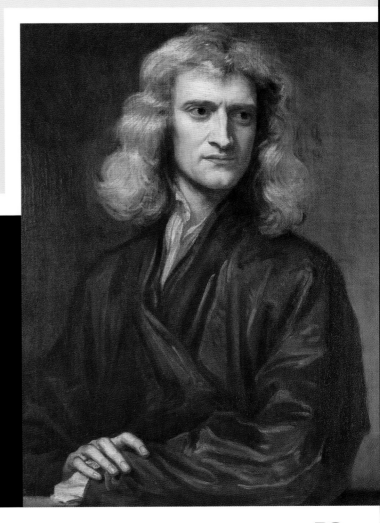

Sir Isaac Newton (right) built the first successful reflecting telescope.

Refraction telescopes are much like powerful magnifying glasses. **Reflecting** telescopes are not as straightforward. They use mirrors rather than **lenses** to focus the image. It took scientists many years to develop and refine reflecting telescopes.

PRIMARIES AND PARABOLAS

Reflecting telescopes use a mirror instead of a lens as an **objective** to gather **visible light.** This **primary mirror** sits at one end of the telescope's tube, where it reflects light that enters the other end of the tube. The primary mirror is curved inward like a bowl. Early mirrors caused some distortion of the image, until scientists began to make mirrors with the curve of a **parabola**. A parabola is a curve like the path of a ball batted high in the air. The parabola is perfectly shaped to direct light to the **focus.**

BOUNCE IT OUT

In Newton's reflector, the image produced by the primary mirror is focused on a flat **secondary mirror,** which bounces it to an **eyepiece** on the side of the telescope. In this way, the open end of the telescope is left clear, so light can pass through to the primary mirror.

REFLECTORS REFINED

In 1672, French telescope maker Guillaume Cassegrain designed a reflector that used a primary mirror with a hole in the center. Light coming into the telescope bounced off the primary mirror to a secondary mirror. While Newton used a flat secondary, Cassegrain used a curved secondary that further focused the image. The image was reflected through a small hole in the primary mirror, with a focus at the end of the telescope tube.

Cassegrain's design is still used in many reflecting telescopes today. Much later it was applied to radio telescopes.

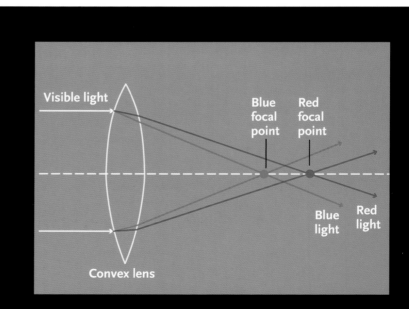

Unlike mirrors, convex lenses cause a color distortion called chromatic aberration in images because different wavelengths come to a focus at separate points.

A reflecting telescope uses mirrors to
gather and focus light from the heavens.

A reflecting telescope's
primary mirror has the
shape of a *parabola*
(a curve like the path
of a ball batted high
in the air).

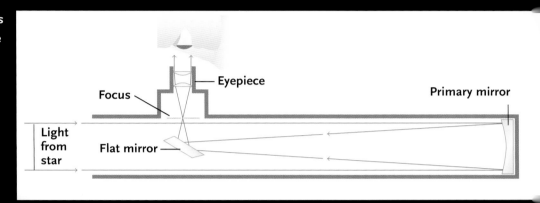

Eyepiece

Focus

Primary mirror

Light
from
star

Flat mirror

Workers polish th
200-inch (5-mete
mirror for the Ha
Telescope in
California in the
1930's. Because
mirrors are thinn
than lenses, they
can be made larg
without sagging
under their own
weight. Polishing
the Hale mirror
took more than
10 years.

HOW DOES A REFLECTING-REFRACTING TELESCOPE WORK?

A third kind of telescope combines aspects of both **reflecting** and **refracting** telescopes. These reflecting-refracting telescopes are also called catadioptric telescopes. An Estonian optician named Bernhard Schmidt invented the catadioptric telescope in 1930.

FROM LENS TO MIRROR

As with other **optical** telescopes, **visible light** enters one end of a reflecting-refracting telescope's tube. The light passes through a **lens** and then strikes a mirror at the far end of the tube. This mirror is *spherical* (shaped like a ball). Light from the primary mirror reflects to a secondary mirror, which focuses the light through a hole in the primary mirror. A reflecting-refracting telescope uses the Cassegrain design in this respect. Astronomers view the image through an **eyepiece.**

COMING INTO FOCUS

Unfortunately, spherical mirrors also distort the image. This distortion is corrected by the lens at the opening of the telescope. The lens bends the incoming light just enough to correct the distortion caused by the spherical mirror.

THE BIG PICTURE

The most important advantage of using a spherical mirror is that it gathers light from a wide field of view. In fact, reflecting-refracting telescopes form images of a larger region of the sky than is possible with any other telescope design. Astronomers have used these telescopes to take photographs of the entire sky. Such photographs are useful for conducting large surveys of **stars.**

Reflecting-refracting telescopes use a combination of lenses and mirrors to gather and focus light.

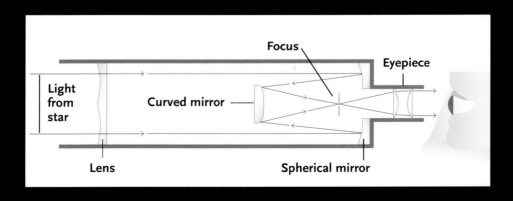

Light from star · Lens · Curved mirror · Focus · Eyepiece · Spherical mirror

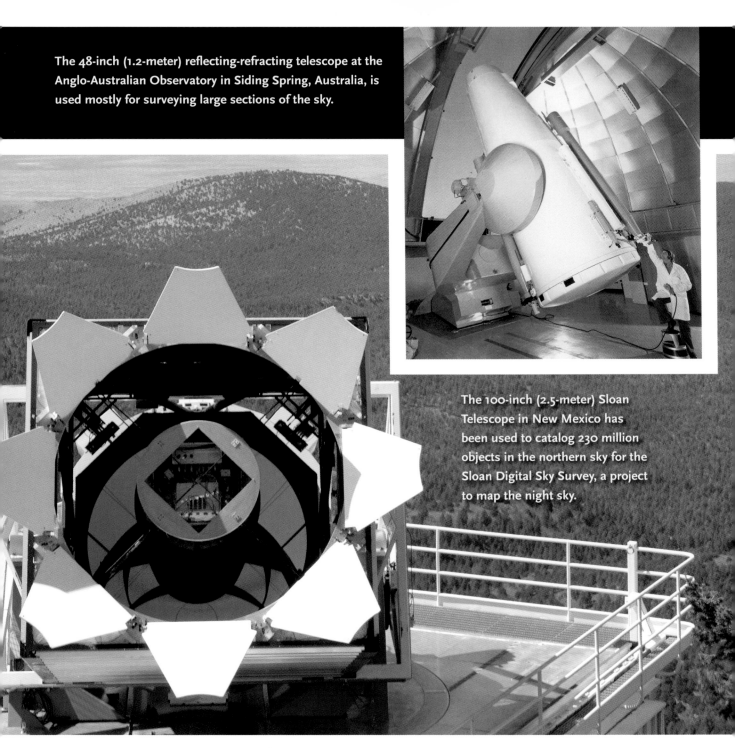

The 48-inch (1.2-meter) reflecting-refracting telescope at the Anglo-Australian Observatory in Siding Spring, Australia, is used mostly for surveying large sections of the sky.

The 100-inch (2.5-meter) Sloan Telescope in New Mexico has been used to catalog 230 million objects in the northern sky for the Sloan Digital Sky Survey, a project to map the night sky.

HOW DO TELESCOPES MAKE IMAGES?

Recording images of the night sky offers many advantages. It allows more than one astronomer to study the same image, sometimes years after the observation. Also, a photograph may be exposed for a long time, which can reveal objects that are too dim to be seen by a person using the telescope directly.

PLATES VS. FILM

Shortly after the invention of photography in the 1800's, astronomers began to fit special camera adaptors to their telescopes. Photography became so important to astronomy that by the mid-1900's, most large telescopes did not even have an **eyepiece.**

The first cameras used bulky glass plates to take photographs. Film soon replaced photographic plates for everyday use, but astronomers continued to use photographic plates as late as the 1990's. Such plates are extremely sensitive to light. They are especially useful for recording large sections of the sky to survey stars.

UNBLINKING EYES

To record light from dim objects, telescopes must track the night sky even as Earth spins. Astronomers place telescopes on a **mounting,** motorized machinery that moves the telescope at the same rate as Earth turns. Computers control the movement, keeping the telescope fixed on an object for as long as desired.

Photographic plates, such as the one used to discover Comet West in 1975 (below), have been replaced by electronics.

DID YOU KNOW?

British-born American chemist John Draper in 1840 became the first scientist to use photography in astronomy when he took the first photograph of the moon.

GOING ELECTRIC

In the 1970's, astronomers began to record images using a **charge-coupled device (CCD)**. CCD's are computer chips that convert light into electrical signals. The same technology may be used in digital cameras, which have largely replaced film cameras in everyday use. CCD's are far more sensitive than film. Also, digital images are easily stored and analyzed by computers. Today, computer technology has replaced older methods of recording images.

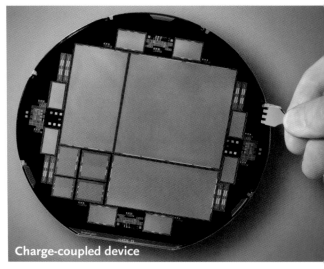

Charge-coupled device

Astronomers aboard a scientifically equipped NASA aircraft in 2006 use a CCD camera to observe the reentry of a space capsule carrying dust from comet Wild-2, captured by the Stardust spacecraft.

HOW DO ASTRONOMERS USE COMPUTERS TO CREATE ASTRONOMICAL IMAGES?

Computers have become important tools in the modern **observatory.** Special chips called **charge-coupled devices (CCD's)** collect even tiny amounts of light from distant **galaxies.** Computers are used to analyze the data generated by CCD's in order to create images. Computers also bring such images to life, helping astronomers to understand what telescopes have observed.

RECORDING LIGHT

Both photographs and CCD's are ways of recording images. The CCD does not generate an image directly. CCD's turn light into an electronic signal, much as a person's optic nerve turns **visible light** collected by our eyes into nerve signals.

Without the human brain, the nerve signals generated by our optic nerve would be meaningless. For telescopes, a computer plays the same basic role as the brain. Electronic signals generated by CCD's take the form of a huge stream of numbers, all zeros and ones. Computers turn the zeros and ones into an image that people can understand.

FALSE COLOR

Infrared and **radio** telescopes capture light that is invisible to our eyes. Because radio waves and infrared light have no natural color, computer programs assign false color to the light collected. The false color is like a translation, expressing information about the light in terms people can understand.

Many of the images recorded by telescopes have little or no color until computers process the data.

A false-color image of Saturn displays information about the size of grains of ice in the planet's rings.

Computer chips can record images directly. Computer programs analyze images and give them color.

BRINGING IT TOGETHER

Computers can also combine observations from different telescopes into a single image. Infrared telescopes penetrate clouds of dust, revealing stars hidden to **optical** telescopes. **X rays** telescopes may reveal especially hot objects that give off little visible light. A computer can combine these images and assign each part of the **spectrum** a distinct color. For example, the computer may display infrared light in red, visible light in yellow, and X rays in blue. Combining different parts of the spectrum in a single image can provide a fuller view of an object in space.

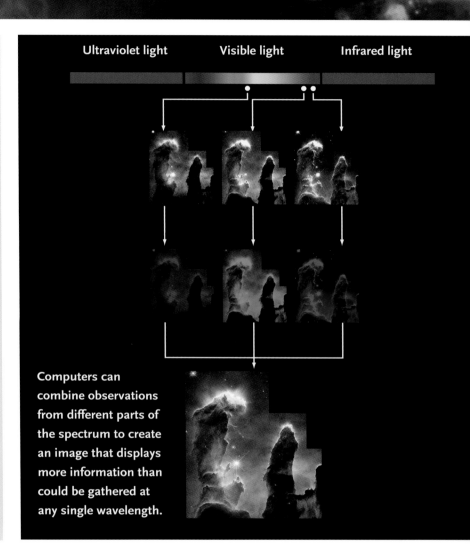

Ultraviolet light   Visible light   Infrared light

Computers can combine observations from different parts of the spectrum to create an image that displays more information than could be gathered at any single wavelength.

DID YOU KNOW?

The "Harvard Computers" were a group of women who, in the late 1800's and early 1900's, catalogued stars and other objects discovered by astronomers using telescopes at Harvard College Observatory in Cambridge, Massachusetts. One of the most famous of these computers was Annie Jump Cannon, who developed a system for classifying more than 35,000 stars.

WHY ARE THERE DIFFERENT KINDS OF TELESCOPE MIRRORS?

For astronomers to build more-powerful telescopes, they must build larger **objective** mirrors. Although mirrors are lighter than **lenses,** the largest mirrors also begin to sag under their own weight. To build more-powerful telescopes, scientists have developed new mirror designs.

BIT BY BIT

Astronomers can link together several small mirrors to act as one large mirror using segmented mirrors. Each of the two Keck telescopes on Mauna Kea in Hawaii has 36 segmented mirrors. Each individual mirror is about 6 feet (1.8 meters) across. Combined, the mirrors equal a reflecting surface 33 feet (10 meters) across. It would be extremely difficult to build a conventional mirror that large.

The Giant Magellan Telescope scheduled for completion in 2018 at Las Campanas, Chile, will collect light using seven 28-foot (8.4-meter) mirrors. These mirrors will combine to act as one mirror 80 feet (24.5 meters) across.

HONEYCOMBS

Honeycomb mirrors are made by pouring molten glass into a mold filled with blocks shaped like the honeycombs in a beehive. These honeycombs give the mirror strength with less weight. In fact, a honeycomb mirror could float on water. Honeycomb mirrors were installed in the Large Binocular Telescope (LBT) in Arizona. Each of the two mirrors in the LBT measures 28 feet (8.4 meters) across.

LIQUID METAL

Liquid mirrors are made of a shiny liquid metal, such as mercury. Electric motors spin a pan filled with liquid metal, giving the metal the proper shape. The shiny liquid metal then acts as a mirror. The Large Zenith Telescope, near Vancouver, Canada, uses a liquid mirror that is about 20 feet (6 meters) across.

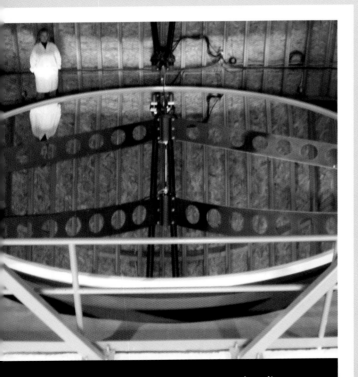

The Large Zenith Telescope in Canada relies on a rotating liquid mirror that is about 20 feet (6 meters) across. The telescope, completed in 2003, is used to study the large-scale structure of the universe and the evolution of galaxies.

To continue increasing the size of objective mirrors, scientists have developed new mirror designs.

Each of the honeycomb mirrors (arrows) in the Large Binocular Telescope in Arizona is 28 feet (8.4 meters) across.

A honeycomb design reduces the weight of a mirror, preventing the mirror from sagging under its own weight.

STARRY SKIES

In order to see the Milky Way as a luminous band of light stretching across the night sky, you need to be far from a city. A person standing in any one place on Earth on a very dark, perfectly clear night can see about 3,000 **stars** without using binoculars or a telescope.

LIGHT AS POLLUTION

The view is different around modern cities. People who live in or near big cities often can see only a handful of stars, even on a clear, moonless night. The problem is **light pollution,** the unwanted illumination of the sky because of human activity. The artificial light from street and highway lights, exterior lights on buildings, lighted billboards, and many other sources in cities "leaks" into the sky. There, it is reflected by dust, water vapor, and other particles in the atmosphere. Bright city lights block starlight in the same way the sun does during the day.

In the night sky over New York City, a person can see only about 25 stars with the unaided eye. About one-fifth of the world's people cannot see the Milky Way without a telescope because of light pollution, according to a 2009 study. This group includes about two-thirds of the population of the United States and one-third of the population of Europe.

A satellite image of North America at night shows how widespread light pollution has become.

In 1908, the Los Angeles area was home to only 350,000 people, and light pollution was only a limited problem for the nearby Mount Wilson Observatory.

Today, more than 9 million people live in the Los Angeles area, and light pollution has become so severe that only the moon and the brightest stars are visible at night.

WHAT HAVE GROUND-BASED OBSERVATORIES TAUGHT US ABOUT THE SOLAR SYSTEM?

Most of the astronomical discoveries that have transformed our view of the universe were made with ground-based **observatories.** In fact, until the 1950's, all observatories were on the ground. The remarkable discoveries made with ground-based observatories begin in our astronomical neighborhood, with the **planets** and other bodies in the **solar system.**

CIRCLING THE SUN

When Galileo studied the heavens with a telescope, he learned that the moon has a rough surface of mountains and craters. He discovered the four largest moons around Jupiter. He became the first astronomer to see Saturn's rings. He also observed that the planet Venus goes through phases, much like Earth's moon.

Galileo's observations confirmed his doubts that Earth was the center of the solar system. He endorsed the findings of Polish astronomer Nicolaus Copernicus, who argued that the sun is the center of the solar system. In this way, ground-based observatories began to transform our view of the universe. Astronomy taught people that Earth is not the center of the universe. Instead, Earth is only one world among many that circle the sun.

Ground-based telescopes enabled astronomers to make out rotating bands of gas in the atmosphere of Jupiter, along with storms as large as Earth.

Telescopes on Earth revealed that comets are actually chunks of ice and dust.

Astronomers using ground-based observatories found all the moons around other planets. They found comets and asteroids, discovered Saturn's rings, and studied the atmosphere of the sun.

ENDLESS MARVELS

Today, ground-based observatories continue to make discoveries about our solar system. There, astronomers track **asteroids.** They study the atmosphere of the sun, learning about solar storms. They observe the moons that orbit Jupiter and Saturn. They peer to the very edges of our solar system, where icy **comets** glide through the void.

Telescopes have allowed astronomers to map the mountains and craters on the moon.

WHAT HAVE GROUND-BASED OBSERVATORIES TAUGHT US ABOUT THE LARGER UNIVERSE?

STELLAR LIFE AND DEATH

Using ground-based observatories, astronomers have observed the births of **stars** in clouds of dust and gas. They have also observed the deaths of stars in violent explosions. Telescopes that "see" **radio waves** revealed the first **pulsars,** which are dead stars that give off light beams like a lighthouse.

Ground-based observatories have revealed a vast universe filled with billions of galaxies. The spiral galaxy IC 342 is 10 million light-years away from Earth.

THE UNIVERSE EXPANDS

In the 1920's, the American astronomer Edwin Hubble proved that there are **galaxies** other than the Milky Way. He also discovered that the universe is expanding. Today, astronomers know that our galaxy is only one of billions in the universe.

THE BIG BANG

In the 1960's, astronomers using radio telescopes discovered evidence that the universe began in an incredible explosion called the **big bang.** Other discoveries support the idea that the universe expanded quickly from a single point, starting 13.7 billion years ago, and that the universe is continuing to expand.

ALIEN LIFE?

Astronomers have found more than 400 worlds circling other stars. Perhaps one day, ground-based observatories will find the first evidence of alien life.

A network of ground-based radio telescopes makes up SETI, the Search for Extraterrestrial Intelligence. The SETI program listens for artificial radio signals from deep space. SETI also uses a network of hundreds of thousands of home computers to sift through the vast amounts of data the program gathers. If SETI finds radio signals from an alien civilization, it will prove that human beings are not the only intelligent life in the galaxy, again changing our view of the universe forever.

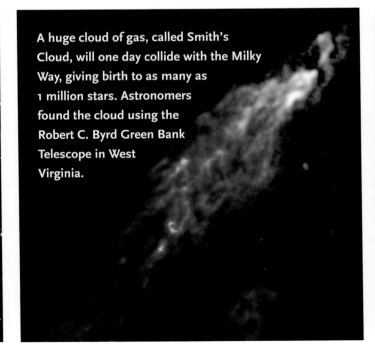

A huge cloud of gas, called Smith's Cloud, will one day collide with the Milky Way, giving birth to as many as 1 million stars. Astronomers found the cloud using the Robert C. Byrd Green Bank Telescope in West Virginia.

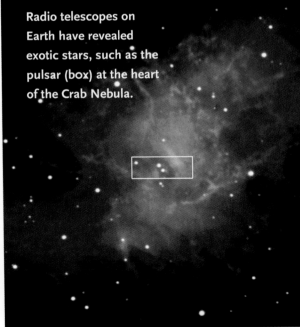

Radio telescopes on Earth have revealed exotic stars, such as the pulsar (box) at the heart of the Crab Nebula.

KITT PEAK OBSERVATORY— AN ASTRONOMICAL OASIS

Kitt Peak National Observatory is located in the Sonoran Desert about 60 miles (95 kilometers) from Tucson, Arizona. The 6,800-foot (2,000-meter) peak is home to 2 radio and 24 optical telescopes, making it one of the most important observatories in the world. The largest of the optical telescopes is the Mayall Telescope. It has a mirror that is 158 inches (4 meters) in diameter.

The National Radio Astronomy Observatory operates one of the radio telescopes at Kitt Peak. With a dish 39 feet (12 meters) in diameter, this telescope collects radio signals in the very short wavelength range. The National Solar Observatory conducts daytime studies of the sun from Kitt Peak.

▲

The most powerful telescope at the Kitt Peak Observatory is the Mayall Telescope. The 18-story telescope can be seen from more than 50 miles (80 kilometers) away. Its protective dome weighs more than 500 tons (454 metric tons). The telescope's primary mirror has a reflective aluminum coating that is only 1/1,000 as thick as a human hair.

The oddly unbalanced spiral galaxy M66, about 35 million light-years from Earth, is one of many galaxies observed from Kitt Peak. Blue and pink areas of this false-color image show areas of star birth.

The Kitt Peak National Observatory in Arizona rises nearly 7,000 feet (2,000 meters) above the Sonoran Desert. The high altitude and dry air minimize atmospheric distortion. The 140-inch (3.5-meter) WIYN Telescope (left in image) is the second largest telescope at Kitt Peak. The Mayall Telescope (right in image) occupies the highest part of the mountain.

WHAT DOES THE FUTURE HOLD FOR GROUND-BASED OBSERVATORIES?

The quest to detect tiny, exotic particles from space called neutrinos has taken astronomers to the bottom of the Homestake gold mine in South Dakota.

Construction has begun on a new generation of ground-based **observatories** that will house telescopes far more powerful than any available today.

COMING ATTRACTIONS

The Giant Magellan Telescope (GMT) in Chile will collect light using seven 28-foot (8.4-meter) mirrors. These **segmented mirrors** will combine to act as one 80-foot-(24.5-meter-) diameter mirror. The GMT is scheduled for completion in 2018.

In 2009, China began construction of a radio telescope called the Five-hundred-meter Aperture Spherical Telescope (FAST). FAST will feature a radio dish 1,640 feet (500 meters) across, equivalent in area to 30 football fields. FAST will become the largest single-dish radio telescope when it is completed in 2014.

EXOTIC OBSERVATORIES

Not all ground-based observatories study light. In 2005, construction began on the IceCube Neutrino Observatory (INO) in Antarctica. INO will detect neutrinos, which are tiny particles born in stars and violent cosmic events. Neutrinos are extremely difficult to detect. In fact, trillions pass through the Earth every second without leaving a trace. Thick ice will shelter INO from interference. It is scheduled for completion in 2011.

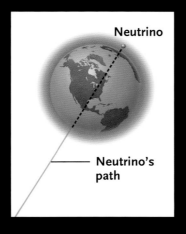

Trillions of neutrinos bombard Earth every second, but nearly all of them pass through without leaving a trace.

Neutrino

Neutrino's path

Several observatories, including the Pierre Auger Observatory in Argentina, are being used to study high-energy cosmic rays. These rays are the most energetic particles in the universe. So far, no one knows for sure where high-energy cosmic rays originate. Scientists hope that studies of these strange particles will one day reveal information about the most extreme parts of the universe.

The Laser Interferometer Gravitational-Wave Observatory (LIGO) detects gravity waves using observatories in Louisiana and Washington. Scientists believe that the most violent events in the universe, such as the explosion of stars, produce these waves. Scientists have begun improvements to LIGO that should greatly increase its sensitivity by 2014.

The Giant Magellan Telescope in Chile (shown in an artist's illustration) will combine seven 28-foot (8.4-meter) mirrors to create the most powerful ground-based telescope ever built.

GLOSSARY

Adaptive optics – A system added to ground-based telescopes to correct for the distorting effects of the atmosphere.

Aperture – The size of the objective lens or mirror in a telescope.

Asteroid – A small, rocky body orbiting around a star.

Atmospheric distortion – The tendency of pockets of moving air and water vapor in Earth's atmosphere to act like lenses, bending light as it travels to the ground. Atmospheric distortion can make objects viewed through a telescope appear blurry.

Big bang – The cosmic explosion that began the expansion of the universe.

Charge-coupled device (CCD) – A computer chip used to record light.

Chemical element – Any substance that contains only one kind of atom. Hydrogen and helium are both chemical elements.

Chromatic aberration – The failure of the different colors of light to meet in one focus when refracted through a convex lens.

Comet – A small, icy body orbiting around a star.

Constellation – A group of stars that resembles a familiar shape in the sky. Astronomers have divided the night sky into 88 constellations, such as Orion (the Hunter).

Convex – A curved surface like the outside of a ball. A convex lens is thickest in the middle and thinnest at its edges.

Electromagnetic radiation – Any form of light, ranging from radio waves, to microwaves, to infrared light, to visible light, to ultraviolet light, to X rays, to gamma rays. Radio waves have the longest wavelength and lowest energy, and gamma rays have the shortest wavelength and highest energy.

Equinox – The time in the fall and spring when the days and nights are of equal length.

Eyepiece – The lens or set of lenses in a telescope that is nearest the eye of the user.

Focal length – The distance from the center of a lens or mirror to the point of focus.

Focus – The point where an image is brought into sharp focus.

Galaxy – A vast system of stars, gas, dust, and other matter held together in space by mutual gravitational attraction.

Gamma rays – The form of light with the shortest wavelengths. Gamma rays are invisible to the unaided eye.

Honeycomb mirror – A mirror made by pouring molten glass into a mold filled with blocks shaped like the honeycombs in a beehive. These honeycombs give the mirror strength with less weight.

Infrared light – A form of light with long wavelengths. Also called heat radiation. Infrared is invisible to the unaided eye.

Lens – A curved piece of glass or other material that gathers and focuses light.

Light pollution – Artificial light that blots out the faint light of stars.

Light-year – The distance light travels in a vacuum in one year. One light-year is equal to 5.88 trillion miles (9.46 trillion kilometers).

Liquid mirror – A mirror made of a shiny liquid metal, such as mercury. Electric motors spin a pan filled with liquid metal, giving the metal the proper shape.

Magnification – The effect whereby objects are made to appear larger.

Mass – The amount of matter in an object.

Microwaves – A kind of radio waves with relatively short wavelengths. Microwaves are invisible to the unaided eye.

Mounting – The machinery that turns a telescope and controls its tilt.

Objective – The large mirror or lens in a telescope that gathers light.

Observatory – A structure used to observe the heavens.

Optical – Of or relating to visible light.

Parabola – A curved shape used in mirrors to bring images into focus.

Planet – A large, round heavenly body that orbits a star.

Primary mirror – The large mirror in a telescope that gathers light. A primary mirror is the objective of a reflecting telescope.

Pulsar – A neutron star that gives off regular pulses of electromagnetic radiation.

Radio waves – The form of light with the longest wavelengths. Radio waves are invisible to the unaided eye.

Reflection – The effect whereby light is thrown back from a mirror.

Refraction – The effect whereby light is turned or bent by a lens.

Resolving power, resolution – The amount of light a telescope gathers. Resolution determines how clear an image will be.

Secondary mirror – A relatively small mirror that reflects light from the primary mirror toward an eyepiece or recording device.

Segmented mirror – A mirror made up of several combined mirrors.

Solar system – The planetary system that includes the sun and Earth.

Solstice – The summer solstice is the longest day of the year. The winter solstice is the shortest day of the year.

Spectrum, spectra – Light divided into its different wavelengths. A spectrum may provide astronomers with information about a heavenly body's chemical composition, motion, and distance.

Spiral galaxy – A galaxy with a thin, disk-like structure and sweeping arms of stars wrapped about the galaxy's center.

Star – A huge, shining ball in space that produces a tremendous amount of light and other forms of energy.

Ultraviolet light – A form of light with short wavelengths. Ultraviolet light is invisible to the unaided eye.

Visible light – The form of light human beings can see with their eyes.

X rays – A form of light with short wavelengths. X rays are invisible to the unaided eye.

Wavelength – The distance between one peak or crest of a wave of light and the next.

FOR MORE INFORMATION

WEB SITES

Ancient Observatories, Timeless Knowledge

http://solar-center.stanford.edu

Look at pictures and read about many of the world's earliest observatories, including those at Chaco Canyon in New Mexico, Stonehenge in England, Angkor Wat in Cambodia, and Machu Picchu in Peru.

Mount Wilson Virtual Tour

http://www.mtwilson.edu

Enter the "Virtual Tour" link to visit Mount Wilson's observatory grounds, including some areas that are closed to the public.

National Solar Observatory

http://www.nso.edu

Information about the telescopes and observatories that the Association of Universities for Research in Astronomy operates in Arizona and New Mexico.

Telescopes from the Ground Up

http://amazing-space.stsci.edu

This feature from the *Amazing Space* Web site follows the history of space observation from the earliest telescopes to NASA's observatories.

BOOKS

Microscopes and Telescopes by Rebecca Stefoff (Benchmark Books, 2007)

More Telescope Power: All New Activities and Projects for Young Astronomers by Gregory L Matloff (John Wiley & Sons, 2002)

Star Spotters: Telescopes and Observatories by David Jefferis (Crabtree Publishing, 2009)

The Telescope by Tamra Orr (Franklin Watts, 2004)

INDEX

ACKNOWLEDGMENTS

The publishers acknowledge the following sources for illustrations. Credits read from top to bottom, left to right, on their respective pages. All illustrations, maps, charts, and diagrams were prepared by the staff unless otherwise noted.

Cover: © Bill Brooks, Masterfile

1   Giant Magellan Telescope - Carnegie Observatories

4-5   © T. W. van Urk, Shutterstock

6-7   WORLD BOOK illustration by Richard Hook; © Andrew Parker, Alamy Images

8-9   Hans A. Rosbach; © Shutterstock; © Chuck Place, Alamy Images; © Alex Neauville, Shutterstock

10-11   Gary Crounse, © Exploratorium (exploratorium.com); © Cosmo Condina Mexico/Alamy Images; © Natalia Bratslavsky, Shutterstock; WORLD BOOK illustration

12-13   © British Library Board/Bridgeman Art Library ; ESO; NOAO/AURA/NSF

14-15   © Shutterstock; © Lance Bellers, Shutterstock; © Shutterstock

16-17   Yuri Beletsky, ESO; NASA; NASA; NASA; Center for Adaptive Optics

18-19   NASA, ESA, CXC, SSC, STSci; Mischa Schirmer/ING, Gilles Bergond/IAA Granada

20-21   WORLD BOOK illustration by Matt Carrington; WORLD BOOK illustration

22-23   NOAO/AURA/NSF; T. A. Rector/Univ. of Alaska Anchorage, T. Abbott and NOAO/AURA/NSF

24-25   Yerkes Observatory Photograph; WORLD BOOK illustration by Leonard E. Morgan; NASA/STSi; Yerkes Observatory Photograph

26-27   California Association for Research in Astronomy/W. M. Keck Observatory; © Jeanne Hatch, Shutterstock; Tom Connell, Wildlife Art/Weldon-Owen, Inc./W. M. Keck Observatory

28-29   © Aaron Kohr, Dreamstime; ESO; © Adam Block, Mt. Lemmon SkyCenter; © Harvard Observatory

30-31   Museo di Fisica e Storia Naturale, Florence, Italy (SCALA/Art Resource); © Bettmann/Corbis

32-33   © Frantzesco Kangaris/EPA/Corbis; Mary Evans Picture Library; NASA

34-35   © John R. Foster, Photo Researchers; WORLD BOOK illustration; WORLD BOOK diagram by Precision Graphics

36-37   Granger Collection; © Emilio Ereza, Alamy Images; © J. R. Eyerman, Time Life Pictures/Getty Images

38-39   WORLD BOOK illustration by Paul D. Turnbaugh; © World History Archive/Alamy Images; WORLD BOOK illustration by Robert Addison; Sir Isaac Newton (1689) by Sir Godfrey Kneller, Uckfield House (© Lebrecht Music & Arts Photo Library/Alamy Images)

40-41   WORLD BOOK illustration; WORLD BOOK illustration; © Peter Stackpole, Time Life Pictures/Getty Images

42-43   WORLD BOOK illustration; Sloan Digital Sky Survey; © Central Press/Getty Images

44-45   ESO; NASA; NASA

46-47   NASA/JPL; NASA; NASA/STSi

48-49   NASA; © Joe McNally, Getty Images; Large Binocular Telescope Observatory

50-51   NASA; The Huntington Library, San Marino, CA; Dave Jurasevich, Mt. Wilson Observatory

52-53   ESO/F. Marchis, M. Wong, E. Marchetti, P. Amico, S. Tordo; T. A. Rector (Univ. of Alaska Anchorage), Z. Levay and L. Frattare (Space Telescope Science Institute) and WIYN/NOAO/AURA/NSF; C. R. Lynds, KPNO/NOAO/NSF

54-55   T. A. Rector/Univ. of Alaska Anchorage, H. Schweiker/WIY and NOAO/AURA/NSF; Bill Saxton, NRAO/AUI/NSF; N. A. Sharp/NOAO/AURA/NSF

56-57   Bill Saxton, NRAO/AUI/NSF; N. A. Sharp/NOAO/AURA/NSF; NOAO/AURA/NSF

58-59   Brookhaven National Laboratory; WORLD BOOK illustration by Roberta Polfus; Giant Magellan Telescope - Carnegie Observatories